INSPIRATIONAL & MOTIVATIONAL
BIBLE VERSE
COLORING BOOK
FOR
Girls

This book is dedicated to my Ezra

Faith Hope Love

1 Corinthians 13:13

Grace and Truth came through Jesus Christ

John 1:17

Rise up & PRAY

LUKE 22:46

God is WITH ME I WILL NOT fail

Psalm 46:5

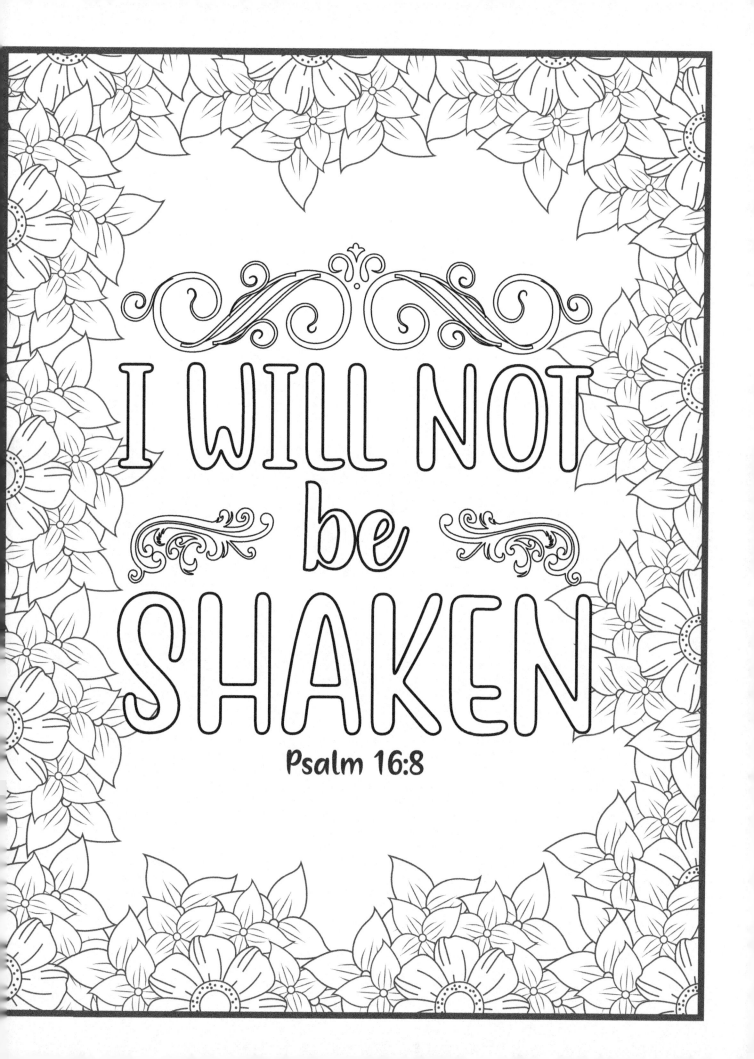

My GRACE is SUFFICIENT for you

2 CORINTHIANS 12:9

Let ALL THAT you DO BE DONE IN Love

1 CORINTHIANS 16:14

I CAN DO all things THROUGH HIM WHO strengthens me

Philippians 4:13

Beauty FROM Ashes

ISAIAH 61:3

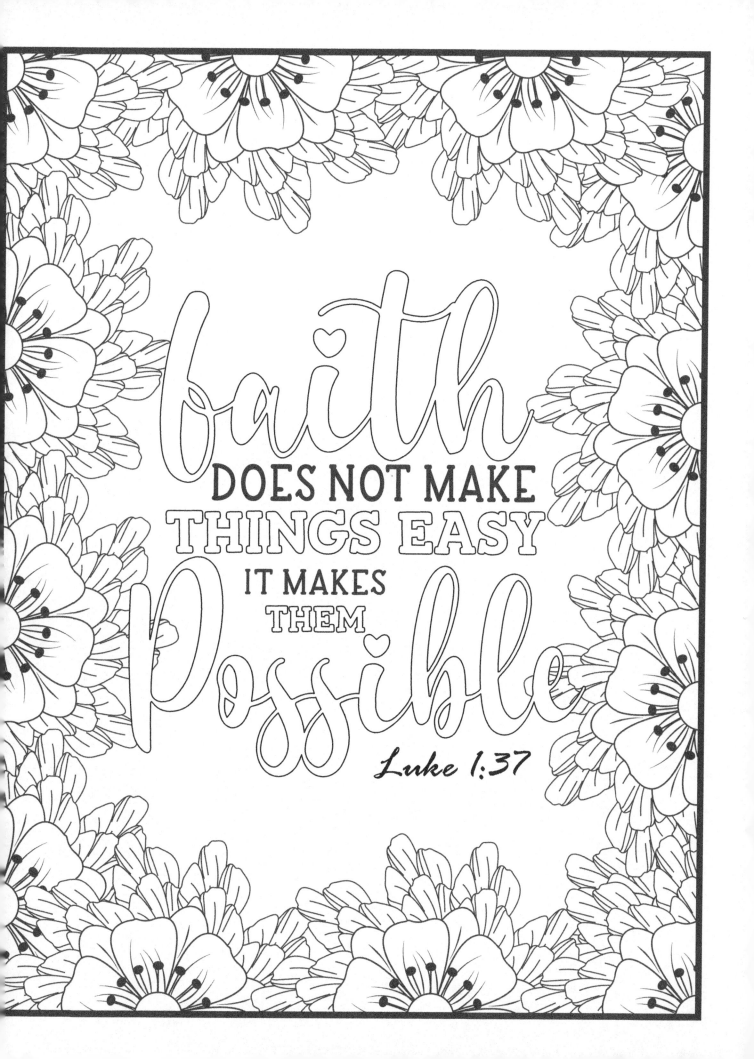

faith
DOES NOT MAKE
THINGS EASY
IT MAKES
THEM
Possible
Luke 1:37

I am FEARFULLY And WONDERFULLY MADE

Psalm 139:14

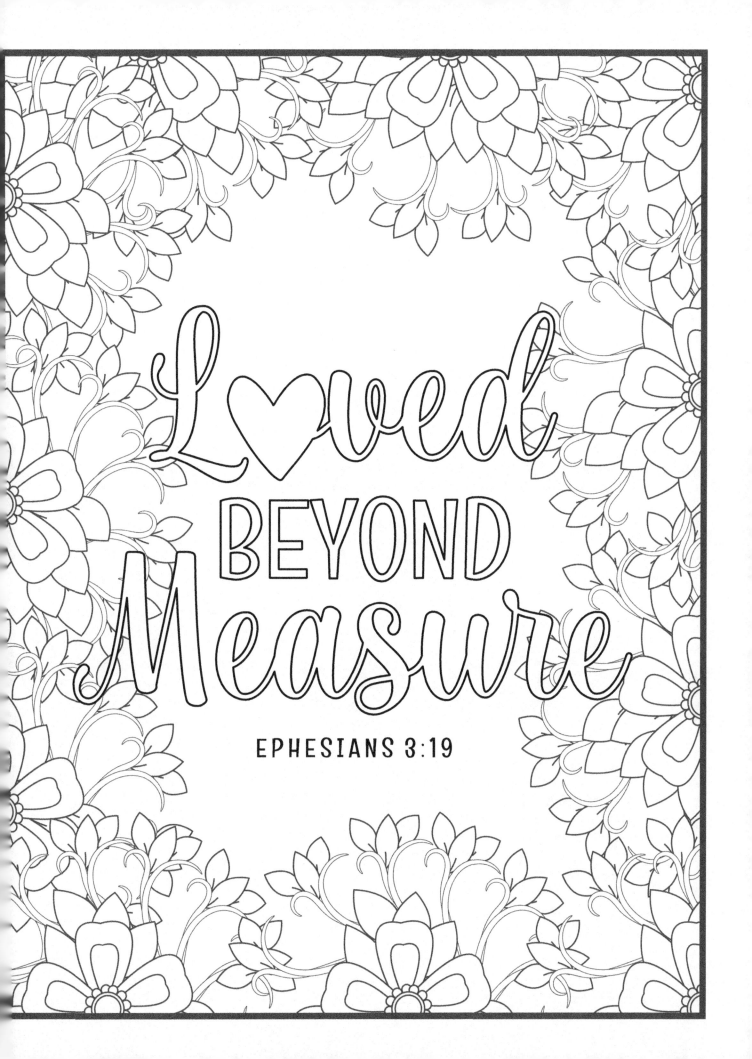

Made in the USA
Las Vegas, NV
27 March 2024

87818097R00044